Original title:
Succulent Sonnets

Copyright © 2025 Creative Arts Management OÜ
All rights reserved.

Author: Elliot Harrison
ISBN HARDBACK: 978-1-80566-593-9
ISBN PAPERBACK: 978-1-80566-878-7

## Heartfelt Bud

In the garden, blooms so sly,
Petals giggle, passersby.
Bees in suits, with ties so neat,
Buzzing gossip, oh so sweet.

Worms in laughter, digging deep,
Tickling roots, lost in sleep.
The sun winks from skies so blue,
While daisies plan a grand debut.

## **Rich Textures**

Leaves are laughing, twist and twirl,
As cacti dance in sandy swirl.
Aloe's spiky, jolly grin,
Teases passersby within.

Fern fronds fan a feathery tease,
Whispering secrets in the breeze.
Mossy carpets, plush and sly,
Invite the critters, oh my, oh my!

## Tapestry of Green

Lush parade, oh how they sway,
Frogs in bowties join the play.
Bumblebees wear hats so grand,
To fashion shows across the land.

Leaves like laughter, bright and bold,
Stories flourish, yet untold.
Underneath the shade, they cheer,
For every bloom that wanders here.

## **Abundant Melodies**

Silly sprouts with tune in heart,
Compose a symphony, a start.
Dripping dew, a drop, a note,
While petals rise and seeds emote.

The wind hums softly, take a bow,
For nature's show is here and now.
Each flower sings, a joyful spree,
Creating laughter, wild and free.

## **Nectar of Dreams**

In a world where daisies wear ties,
And tulips tell jests 'neath the skies,
The bees hold a court, so absurd,
As daisies dance, with laughter unheard.

Night brings a moonlit bouquet,
Where roses gossip, hip-hip hooray!
The petals quibble, what a fine jest,
In dreams made of nectar, we find our best.

**Petals of Passion**

A daffodil claims it can tap dance,
While violets plot love at a glance.
The pansies chuckle, oh what a play,
As bees serve tea, in their own way.

Sweet aromas tumble and twirl,
As sunflowers flirt, oh don't you swirl!
With petals that blush and giggle, oh dear,
In this garden of hearts, let's spread some cheer.

## **Garden of Stanzas**

We planted a verse near the old oak,
Where rhymes grow wild, and laughter spoke.
The marigolds jest, while ferns high-five,
In this plot of poetry, we come alive.

Every bloom holds a story to tell,
From silly haikus to sonnets that swell.
They dance in the breeze, oh such a sight,
In this garden of lines, we bask in delight.

**Verdant Whispers**

The grass has secrets, soft and sly,
While lilacs plot mischief nearby.
With whispers of joy in the rustling leaves,
Nature's humor always deceives.

As clovers giggle in the sweet shade,
And ferns exchange tips on how to invade,
A tapestry of chuckles we weave,
In verdant realms, oh how we believe.

## **Vivid Landscapes**

In a garden so bright, the colors collide,
With tomatoes that dance in a juicy red tide.
The carrots wear hats, oh the silly sight,
While lettuce sings songs under the moonlight.

A radish once dreamed it could fly like a kite,
But tripped on a weed and gave up the fight.
With laughter we pluck, it's a comical scene,
Our veggies unite in the happiest green.

## **Verdure in Verses**

Broccoli giggles, it's not very cool,
While peas play hide and seek in a pool.
The onions, they cry, but it's tears of good cheer,
Throwing a party for vegetables here!

The garlic shakes hands, oh what a delight,
As spinach debates if it's ready for flight.
Their leaves twirl and tangle in joyful embrace,
In this veggie fiesta, let's pick up the pace!

**Breathe the Soil**

Under the surface, worms tell a tale,
Of plants growing wild in their grand leafy trail.
They chuckle and wiggle, in dirt they delight,
"Just give us some rain, and we'll dance through the night!"

Potatoes sit out, tired of hiding,
While radish roots play games with the gliding.
The herbs make a ruckus, a fragrant parade,
In this wacky garden, where fun's never delayed.

**Thriving Thoughts**

In pots filled with dreams and quirky delight,
The cactus throws parties, spikes glittering bright.
A sunflower whispers sweet nonsense in mid,
While marigolds giggle, and that's just the bid.

Basil's a poet, rosemary's wise,
Mints are the jokers with sparkling eyes.
Together they flourish, they thrive and they jest,
In this magical patch, we're truly blessed!

## Sweet Syllables

Bantering blooms in the garden so bright,
With giggles of daisies that giggle at night.
The roses wear hats that are quite out of date,
While tulips are gossiping, oh what a fate!

Silly petals flutter, like they're at a ball,
They're dancing with breezes, not caring at all.
Their laughter, a melody carried on air,
As flowers exchange tales of blunders they share.

## **Flourishing Lines**

In sunlit patches, where jokes blossom free,
The carrots are cracking up, can't you see?
The lettuce is laughing, all crisp and divine,
While peas in their pods form a comical line.

The beets tell a story that's fabled and grand,
While radishes blush at the jokes they had planned.
Each sprout brings a smile, a quirk of design,
In rows that are bursting with punchlines so fine.

## **Vivid Blooms**

Chortling flowers with colors so wild,
Sunflowers chuckle, they're nature's own child.
Petunias wear shades of the silliest hues,
While lilacs spread gossip like they're in the news.

The zinnias bounce with a humorous grace,
As marigolds poke fun at their own silly face.
In this painting of laughter, so vivid and bright,
Nature's own canvas brings joy to our sight.

## Aroma of Elegy

In gardens of whimsy, their scents intertwine,
With giggles of blossoms and jokes that align.
The lilies, though solemn, can't help but snicker,
While violets tease, their humor's quite slicker.

Daisies declare it's a riotous time,
As petunias recite a not-so-funny rhyme.
Even the willows sway in laughter's embrace,
In the aroma of mischief, we find our own place.

## **Botanical Ballads**

In gardens where the lettuce sings,
I found a bee wearing tiny rings.
It danced atop the daisies bright,
And sipped sweet nectar day and night.

The carrots wear a leafy crown,
While radishes all joke around.
The broccoli tells knock-knock jokes,
While peas roll laughing like sweet folks.

Sunflowers strut with proud display,
While roses blush in bright array.
Each plant has stories, oh so grand,
In this green realm, we're hand in hand.

The thyme insists on telling tales,
About the herbs and their grand trails.
With giggles shared beneath the sun,
Botanical ballads are such fun!

**Blossoms of the Heart**

Roses whisper secrets of love,
While daisies fall from skies above.
Each petal giggles, loose and free,
In this garden, you'll feel the glee.

Tulips twirl in a sunlit dance,
With daisies dreaming of romance.
The violets peep, so shy and sweet,
Their laughter brings the world to feet.

A dandelion sneezes with cheer,
Spreading wishes both far and near.
The lilies clap their lovely hands,
As bees all gather in joyful bands.

Under stars, the flowers conspire,
Crafting jokes to lift hearts higher.
In blossoms, we find joy and mirth,
Echoes of laughter throughout the earth!

## **Lush Verses**

In fields where squash and pumpkins grow,
They tell tall tales with a playful glow.
The zucchini laughs as it stretches wide,
With cucumbers joining for the ride.

The peppers sing a spicy tune,
While corn kernels sway beneath the moon.
Each veggie jests, it's quite the sight,
In this garden, there's pure delight.

The radishes wear sunglasses cool,
While carrots hold a vibrant school.
With each fresh bloom that starts to sprout,
The jokes keep growing, there's no doubt.

The lettuce conducts a leafy choir,
While onions play the dreaded liar.
In lush verses, let's share a grin,
For nature's humor is where we begin!

## Juicy Rhymes

The fruits all gather, ripe and round,
With laughter bursting at every sound.
The oranges tease with zesty flair,
While cherries giggle, without a care.

The grapes are tangled in a mess,
Swapping stories, they're quite the press.
Bananas slip on peels of wit,
In fruity jokes, they all commit.

The melons throw a summer bash,
With berry drinks that blend and splash.
Each juicy rhyme is sweetly spun,
As laughter ripens, oh what fun!

In this garden, humor flows,
In every bite, a punchline grows.
So join the fruits, let's laugh and play,
For juicy rhymes are here to stay!

## **A Bounty of Beauty**

In my garden, tomatoes wear hats,
Peppers dance like giggling cats.
Carrots hide beneath leafy crowns,
In the midst of chuckles, no frowns.

Zucchinis play peek-a-boo, oh dear,
Knocking on doors, drawing near.
Radishes roll in their spicy beds,
Tickling others with their bright reds.

The cucumbers launch a comedy show,
With punchlines that make the sprouts go "Whoa!"
Lettuce winks with a crunchy grin,
As herbs gossip about where they've been.

In this patch, humor really grows,
Thanks to the laughter that everyone knows.
Each veggie's a jester, taking the lead,
In a landscape of joy, with every seed.

## A Symphony of Growth

In the soil, a melody plays,
Roots twist and turn in silly ways.
A trumpet plant toots through the night,
While daisies tango, what a sight!

The sunflowers sway, conducting the show,
With bees in tuxedos, they steal the flow.
Raindrops keep tapping, a rhythm divine,
While mushrooms throw parties with wild wine.

Sprouts burst forth, in sequins so bright,
Performing a jig under the moonlight.
With each little bud, the laughter expands,
In this orchestra, joy takes a stand.

Nature's a clown, with antics galore,
Each plant adds humor, who could ask for more?
So grab your earplugs and join this ride,
In the symphonic garden, let laughter guide.

## Ephemeral Garden

In my fleeting garden, nothing's quite still,
A flower sneezes, it's quite the thrill.
With petals that flutter and giggle away,
Each bright little bloom wants to play.

The dandelions puff in playful jest,
As bees buzz around in a zany quest.
With every new bud, a joke blooms anew,
Like poppies in suits, twirling just for you.

But alas, the petals fall with a smile,
Dancing in breezes, they stretch for a mile.
With every goodbye, a chuckle remains,
In this ephemeral land, joy still reigns.

So here's to the flowers, brief but so bold,
Spreading laughter like stories told.
In a garden of giggles, don't miss your chance,
To waltz with the weeds in this whimsical dance.

## Rhythmic Blossoming

In a world where daisies moonwalk and sway,
Forget clapping hands, watch how flowers play.
Budding roses wear shades, ready to groove,
As the tulips shake it, finding their move.

Petunias sport sneakers, ready to jam,
While sunflowers spin, what a grand slam.
The daisies giggle, spinning around,
Creating a fiesta right on the ground.

With each rhythmic blossom, life's a delight,
They chirp and they chuckle, keeping it light.
Pollens are confetti, swirling through air,
In this rhythmic garden, joy is everywhere.

So dance with the blossoms, let laughter ignite,
In this flowered ruckus, everything's right.
Each bloom's a comedian, wild and free,
In the garden's embrace, come laugh with me!

## Enchanted Roots

In a garden where gnomes read their books,
The carrots wear sunglasses, and thyme just cooks.
Radishes dance with a jig and a twist,
While talking to beans, and none can resist.

The turnips are chatting, oh what a scene,
They gossip like kids, bright-eyed and keen.
With cucumbers laughing and pumpkins that cheer,
They throw a big party as spring draws near.

In the soil, they giggle, sharing their dreams,
While onions in layers pull off clever schemes.
The radicchio's prance in a ruffled ballet,
While spinach just sighs, "What a fabulous day!"

As dawn breaks, the garden throws back its head,
And sprouts play tag with the sun overhead.
With roots deep in joy, they flourish their way,
In this nonsense realm where veggies love play.

## Harmonies of Harvest

In fields where the tomatoes wear hats quite profound,
A symphony's brewing, strange melodies found.
Cucumbers jamming on strings made of twine,
While the sweet corn hums a tune, oh so fine.

The beets keep the rhythm, they thump and they pluck,
But jalapeños scream, "Not a whole lot of luck!"
With carrots on drums, and peas in a band,
They rock the whole plot, with a twist and a stand.

The sunflowers dance with their heads raised up high,
While lettuce in layers thinks it's too shy.
Zucchini joins in with a little grand flair,
As veggies unite in the harvest parade.

With laughter and music, they all play their part,
In this vibrant garden, where joy's a fine art.
So if you hear laughter when you stroll on through,
It's just veggies serenading for you, yes, you!

## **Silken Leaf Lyrics**

In the orchard of dreams where the mint leaves sway,
The chives tell tall tales in a breezy display.
Elfin pears giggle, while apples keep score,
As strawberries flirt with their sweetness galore.

Avocados compose with a rhythm so rare,
While herbs spin their yarns with a whimsical flair.
The basil is bold, with a voice oh so light,
While parsley pirouettes, all dressed up for the night.

From thyme to cilantro, they sing to the moon,
Through breezy ballets, in whimsical tune.
With lettuce in layers, all draped in sheer silk,
They twirl through the garden, sweet dreams made of milk.

And when morning breaks down with dew on the ground,

The leaves weave their stories, a soft, gentle sound.
With laughter and joy, they embrace the day's light,
In this garden of verses, a fun-filled delight.

## Fruits of Inspiration

In a bowl full of colors, the fruits start to plot,
A conference of flavors, all stretching their thought.
Bananas crack jokes as they swing in the air,
While oranges ponder, "Is it worth all this care?"

The apples are hearty, with wisdom to share,
But grapefruits just giggle, with zest everywhere.
Mangoes play tricks, oh they're quite the tease,
And cherries just bounce with the greatest of ease.

Their skins shine like jewels, in the sun's golden glow,
As peaches recite their best lines in a row.
"Be fruity!" they chant, "And let laughter ignite,
In the garden of joy, everything feels right!"

With every sweet bite, there's a chuckle in store,
In this fruity fiesta, who could ask for more?
So gather round folks, let's celebrate cheer,
With fruits as our friends, let's shout loud and clear!

## Wild Harvest

In a garden lush, weeds take a stance,
They dance a jig, it's a weedy romance.
Tomatoes giggle, under sun's warm glow,
While carrots play hide and seek, just so.

Pumpkins plot mischief, round and so bright,
Whispering secrets in the pale moonlight.
A farmer chuckles, he's seen it before,
His veggies a circus, oh what a score!

## **Botanical Ballad**

Oh, the herbs in the kitchen have started to sing,
Basil's a diva, with flair and bling.
Thyme's always on time, with jokes at the ready,
Sage makes the puns—his humor is steady.

Parsley prances, oh what a sight,
Onions cry laughter, but they smell just right.
Garlic makes faces, trying to compete,
In this botanical play, oh, isn't it sweet!

## Ornate Odes

A rose in a vase with a dramatic flair,
Complains about thorns, 'Life's just not fair!'
Daisies roll 'round, laughing with glee,
While lilies pose grandly, as silly as can be.

Tulips march proudly in a vibrant array,
Declaring the garden their bright cabaret.
Chrysanthemums giggle, with petals so round,
In this flowery fest, silliness abounds!

## **Verdant Revelations**

In leaves of green, mischief does sprout,
Cucumbers whisper, 'What's this about?'
Lettuce declares with a crisp, loud crunch,
And radishes giggle, all ready to brunch.

Beans tell tall tales, they stretch to the sky,
While zucchini flexes, oh my, oh my!
Corn takes a bow, with its husky old charm,
Fruits and veggies plotting, oh, what a farm!

## **Tangy Tales**

In a garden where lemons play,
Grapefruits gossip, night and day.
Limes do cartwheels, what a sight,
Even oranges wear hats so bright.

Peppers pirouette, beans tap dance,
Carrots in tuxedos, take a chance.
Radishes laugh, and onions cry,
Broccoli spins, oh my, oh my!

The peas all chuckle, a snicker here,
While cabbage heads roll in good cheer.
Tomatoes wink with secret glee,
In this funny patch, all are free.

So join the feast, no need to pout,
With veggie jokes, there's never doubt.
A tangy tale crafted with fun,
In this zany garden, laughter's won!

## Bountiful Breaths

In a world where spinach sings,
Kale wears crowns and jolly swings.
Parsley prances, what a twirl,
Garlic jokes, it makes us whirl.

Radishes act like kings and queens,
While beets flaunt their ruby sheens.
Chickpeas chuckle, beans just grin,
Lentils tease, 'Come join our spin!'

Gourds do ballet, oh such grace,
Pumpkins pose, brightening the place.
In this party of veggie cheer,
Every breath brings laughter near.

So take a moment, breathe it in,
This bounty of wit, let the fun begin.
With every crunch, there's joy to find,
Laughing roots, oh what a bind!

# **Radiant Imagery**

A salsa dance of colors bright,
Tomatoes wear shades, feeling light.
Cilantro twirls with fragrant flair,
Basil grins, waving in the air.

Carrots do the cha-cha slide,
While onions dally, full of pride.
Peppers shimmy, making a scene,
In this garden, we're all keen.

Snap peas laugh, and eggplants cheer,
Corn pops by, spreading good cheer.
Radicchio rolls, what a delight,
Vegetable antics, pure and bright!

Imagine a world where veggies play,
Every moment's a holiday.
With radiant smiles and goofy grins,
In this lush land, the fun begins!

## Blossom in Rhyme

A flower's tale in a sunny nook,
Daisies dance as the bumblebees look.
Roses tickle, their petals spin,
Laughing loudly, they let joy in.

Tulips joke, with colors so bold,
Sunflowers tease, a sight to behold.
Violets chuckle, whispering soft,
In this garden, they twirl aloft.

Pansies giggle, the daisies sigh,
Petunias burst with laughter nearby.
Every bloom a joke to share,
In this bright patch, we shed all care.

So bring your smiles, come take a peek,
In this flowered realm, we'll laugh and speak.
To blossom in rhyme, take a step,
A garden await, with joy adept!

## Opulent Muses

A cactus wearing shoes, oh dear,
It spins and twirls with cheer.
Each spiny poke a laugh might bring,
Who knew that plants could dance and sing?

The tulips blush in bright array,
As bumblebees join in the play.
With petals wide, they shout with glee,
"Oh, come and sip our honey tea!"

A gnome with socks that do not match,
Contemplates his little patch.
He tells a joke to laughing vines,
The sun chuckles, its warmth entwines.

A rose with shades of neon pink,
Makes passes at a garden sink.
They share a sip, oh what a sight,
As fireflies join in the night!

## Whimsical Flora

Daisy wears a polka dot tie,
While dandelions wave goodbye.
A moonbeam slides upon the scene,
As daisies giggle, feeling keen.

The violets in their frocks of blue,
Tell silly tales of morning dew.
While the sunflowers boast, oh so proud,
Claiming they're the best, so loud!

A tulip gives a cheeky wink,
To bees who buzz and softly blink.
With petals soft like beds of fluff,
They giggle, saying, "Is that enough?"

In this garden where jesters reign,
Even weeds jump up and entertain.
Among the blooms, such joy is found,
As laughter dances 'round and 'round!

## Harvest Moon Musings

The pumpkins wear a silly grin,
As squash chased corn, that cheeky kin.
Under the moon that breaks the night,
They wish they had a chance to flight.

The scarecrow joins with floppy hat,
And draws a smile from a sleeping cat.
They share a secret, soft and sweet,
Portraying tales of plants discreet.

Corn husks rustle, gossip flies,
While crickets play their lullabies.
With every nutty, crunchy sound,
The laughs of harvest can be found.

As twilight wraps the fields with glee,
The fruits dance joyfully, carefree.
In the night of shadows, blooms cast light,
Oh, what fun beneath the starlight!

## Lush Landscapes

In jungles deep, the ferns take flight,
As parrots crack jokes, oh what a sight!
They swing from branches, full of flair,
With elephant friends, they dance with care.

A hydrangea with a hefty hat,
Tells gossipy tales to a curious cat.
In the sun-kissed glades, laughter rings,
As flowers play and nature sings.

The willows dip their leafy toes,
In rivers where the laughter flows.
Swaying sweetly, they join the beat,
As turtles tap dance, soft and fleet.

In vibrant hues, this landscape beams,
Where nature lives and dances in dreams.
With humor drawn from verdant streams,
Life's a party, bursting at the seams!

## Bounty of Blooms

In gardens bright, so lush and chime,
The daisies dance, a wobbly mime.
With roses blushing, oh what a sight,
They giggle loud in the morning light.

The sunflowers nod, with heads so grand,
As bees in suits shake tiny hands.
Petals whisper secrets, oh so sly,
While butterflies flutter, as if to fly.

With every bud, a joke unwinds,
In nature's jest, laughter binds.
The tulips twirl in a jolly spree,
Nature's comedy, come join the glee!

So raise a cup to blooms galore,
For every flower has tales to score!
In this plot of joy, just don't get stuck,
In the prickle of roses—oh, what bad luck!

## Savoring Sweetness

Oh, the nectar drips like honeyed dreams,
As bees conspire with sugary schemes.
Petals blush with laughter on high,
While ants march forth, never asking why.

Taste the essence made just for fun,
As butterflies flutter in the sun.
They sip and swirl, a dance divine,
A sweet ballet in nature's vine.

Daisies giggle, 'Have a bite!'
As bees buzz round in sheer delight.
The sweetness spreads from bloom to bloom,
A feasting surely will bring room!

So join the feast, don't be too shy,
In floral laughter, we just can't lie!
In fields of joy, life's a tasty treat,
We'll savor sweetness, can't be beat!

## **Floral Serenade**

In a garden lush, where petals sing,
The lollygagging blooms do their thing.
A daffodil winks with a golden grin,
While ladybugs dance, let the giggles begin!

Each flower sways to a merry tune,
Under the watch of the silly moon.
The violets whisper, 'What's the joke?'
As starlings chuckle, with every poke.

Tulips tease with their vibrant flair,
As blossoms gossip, without a care.
This floral choir brings joy anew,
In laughter's embrace, there's always a crew!

So join the song, let your cares be few,
The flora knows what life's meant to do.
In the symphony of colors that play,
The floral serenade will rule the day!

## **Nectar's Embrace**

In a world of colors, so bright and clear,
Nectar's embrace brings us good cheer.
The blooms are giggling, a sight to see,
As bees hum softly, sipping with glee.

Lavender laughs as it sways in the breeze,
While violets plot silly mischief with ease.
Petals whisper tunes, like secrets in rhyme,
Celebrating joy, one flower at a time.

A joyful thistle, though prickly and shy,
Spins tales of sweetness, oh my, oh my!
The daisies chuckling at dandelion dreams,
Under the sun, laughter's sunbeams.

So cherish the nectar, every sweet drop,
In this floral carnival, we'll dance and bop!
With nectar's embrace, let your spirits soar,
In this flower-filled life, always ask for more!

## Savoring Stanzas

In a garden where pickles grow tall,
Lettuce laughs, oh it's quite the ball!
Tomatoes dance in the sunshine broad,
While onions sing in a vegetable clod.

Cucumbers twirl, so cool and slick,
Carrots giggle, what a funny trick!
Peppers prance in their vibrant hues,
While garlic whispers old trade news.

Beets wear hats made of leafy green,
In this patch, a comical scene!
Radishes joke about their red hue,
In this quirky crew, what will they do?

So come join in, don't be a bore,
Let's dance with veggies, forevermore!
A feast of laughs on a joyous plate,
Where every bite is a giggly fate.

**Tangible Tranquility**


In a patch of thyme that's quite bizarre,
A carrot dreams of being a star.
It whispers low to the sage so wise,
"Do you think I'll get some surprise?"

The broccoli, proud, gives a hearty shout,
"Let's throw a party, make no doubt!"
And so the peas wear party hats,
Counting their friends, all merry chitchats.

The peppers argue 'bout who's the spiciest,
While squash joins in, feeling quite dicey.
Tomatoes roll in with a jolly cheer,
"Lettuce, my friend, we're the life here!"

As worms dance a jig in soft soil bed,
The world's a buffet of laughs, it's said.
A tip of the hat to the garden crew,
Where joy sprouts up like morning dew!

**Blooms of Serenity**

In a meadow full of giggling flowers,
Sunlight sips from the showering hours.
Daisies swap tales with a bold sunflower,
While bees buzz in with a workload to scour.

Roses roll their eyes at the tulips' show,
"Your flamboyance could really steal the glow!"
Lilies chuckle, quite serene and bright,
"Let's all just smile, it's a funny sight!"

Buttercups flutter, adorned with glee,
"Who's the fairest? Come, stand by me!"
With petals dancing in breezy delight,
The flowers giggle through day and night.

In this botanical fiesta, chaos rules,
As blossoms plot like mischievous fools.
With each little laugh, they twine and sway,
In the world of blooms, it's a comedy play!

**Rhymes in the Meadow**

In a meadow of rhymes, weeds wear tall hats,
While butterflies bounce, avoiding the chats.
The daisies jest about the bees' sweet flight,
"Let's throw a gala, make it a night!"

The grasses sway in a line dance near,
As crickets play tunes for all to hear.
Ladybugs giggle and wiggle on leaves,
Rabbits hop in, with trickster reprieves.

The sunflowers jest, a sight grand and bright,
"Who wore it best in this wild delight?"
With petals pointing and laughter galore,
This meadow is fun, who could ask for more?

So come join the fun, let's all take a peek,
This meadow is jolly, and far from bleak.
With nature's own humor, let spirits soar,
In the heart of this place, life's a laughter store!

# Repose in Petals

In gardens where the daisies play,
I found a snail who went astray.
He waved a leaf, said, "Do not fret!"
"I'm off to see a sunset!"

With every step, he leaves a trail,
A slimy map, but don't inhale!
He dreams of flying, oh so grand,
His little legs, they just can't stand!

A ladybug gave him a wink,
"With legs so tiny, don't you think?"
The snail just laughed, "I'll run the race!"
At that, he tumbled, fell from grace!

Yet every bloom cheered on his quest,
And nature giggled, feeling blessed.
For every bloom, and every pest,
Can't help but join in friendship's jest.

## Nature's Sweet Canvas

The squirrels paint with acorn caps,
While birds compose their chirpy raps.
A canvas made of leaf and stone,
With every color, nature's own!

The bees are busy, buzzing loud,
Creating works that make them proud.
"Check my masterpiece!" one exclaimed,
"Just watch me dance, I won't be tamed!"

The flowers giggle, swaying side,
While butterflies take them for a ride.
A rainbow palette, sunlit cheer,
Nature's art, the world's best beer!

The trees perform a leafy twist,
With every breeze, they can't resist.
In humorous strokes, they find their flair,
A joyful gallery beyond compare.

## Lyrical Landscapes

Oh sing a tune of rolling hills,
Where cows create their own goodwill.
A sheep began to strut and dance,
They called it 'Baa-rry's big romance!'

The brook, it chuckles, bubbling clear,
When frogs join in with songs to cheer.
They croak their rhymes till dusk is nigh,
While owls hoot out, "Just let it fly!"

Each flower dances in the breeze,
With petals swaying like it's cheese.
A dandelion sneezes with glee,
"Watch out world, I'm free as can be!"

So let's create our joyous tune,
In landscapes where we mime the moon.
With laughter painting nature's scene,
Life's a canvas, bright and keen!

## Bursting Blossoms

The tulips wore their hats askew,
And laughed aloud, "Hey, how about you?"
A daffodil chimed in with flair,
"Let's host a party, come if you dare!"

Cherries giggled, pendulous and red,
While peas in pods danced right ahead.
"Join us for a juicy feast!"
"Let's celebrate, our crops increased!"

Yet pesky wasp flew overhead,
Demanding sweets, by nectar fed.
The flowers huddled, what a sight,
"Buzz off, dear friend, this isn't right!"

In bursts of laughter, blooms converge,
With petals flaring, they emerge.
For every stem that bends in mirth,
A hint of joy brings life to earth.

## Dreaming in Full Bloom

In gardens where the roses tease,
A squirrel shimmies with such ease,
He's got his shades and fancy shoes,
Dancing 'round like he just can't lose.

The daisies giggle, oh what a sight,
As bumblebees plan to take flight,
A daisy whispers to her friend,
'If he trips now, it'll be the end!'

With petals soft and whispers sweet,
They plot to serve him something neat,
A cupcake topped with sprightly sprout,
"Who knew this garden's full of clout?"

So here's to blooms with funny ways,
Who turn our frowns to sunny rays,
In dreamland where the wild things bloom,
We laugh our way through nature's room.

## The Color of Breath

A rainbow sneezed, what a surprise,
And out popped colors from the skies,
The clouds all giggled as they passed,
While windshields sparkled, dreams amassed.

Lemonade bursts in shades so bright,
While cheeky breezes take a bite,
Of flavored clouds that taste like cheese,
They're laughing all in perfect ease.

How odd to see a windy flare,
As laughter lifts the heavy air,
Dancing shades of orange and blue,
Who knew that breath could paint anew?

So catch a whiff of breezy cheer,
Where colors change and laughter's near,
In a world where breath inspires,
A palette of delight that never tires.

## Aroma of Echoes

In forests deep where giggles grow,
The echo's voice begins to flow,
A whiff of mint and lavender,
As trees conspire and murmur blur.

"Did you hear that?" a pine tree said,
"I think I saw a squirrel fled!"
Echo replied with a chuckle loud,
"Let's play hide and seek, we're so proud!"

The aroma of mischief in the air,
As flourished ferns discuss with flair,
Each twirl and twist inspires delight,
In their woodland ballet, a funny sight.

So let the echoes rise and cheer,
With scents that charm and dance so near,
In nature's prank, where laughs collide,
A funny dream, nowhere to hide.

## **Dew-Kissed Delights**

Morning dew on petals fine,
A slippery slide, but oh, divine!
The ladybugs choose to bop,
While snails get dizzy when they stop.

Mischief brews in every drop,
As butterflies take a joyful hop,
The daisies flutter and start to sway,
Singing songs in a humorous way.

Each droplet holds a little jest,
As ants create a funny quest,
"Who pipped the toast?" they shout with glee,
While sipping nectar like it's tea.

So taste the morning, fresh and bright,
With dew-kissed giggles on the right,
In nature's garden, life takes flight,
And laughter lingers, pure delight.

# Echoes of the Orchard

In the orchard where fruits giggle,
Apples tease with their shiny wiggle.
Peaches parade in a fuzzy throng,
While cherries burst out in a fruity song.

Grapes gossip in clusters, oh so sly,
Making puns as the bees buzz by.
Lemons roll eyes, they think they're zest,
While oranges claim to be the best.

The pears are laughing, full of cheer,
Waving to folks who come near.
Under the branches, joy takes flight,
As fruits laugh on through day and night.

So if you're feeling a little blue,
Join the fun in the orchard, too!
Laughter's ripe and waiting for all,
With giggling fruits, you'll have a ball.

## Soft Embrace of Language

Words flutter like butterflies in spring,
Tickling your ears, making hearts sing.
Puns bounce around like playful kids,
While metaphors dance, and reason skids.

Every whisper carries a chuckling hint,
As similes giggle and meanings glint.
Language is soft, yet wildly absurd,
A playful chaos in every word.

Tongue twisters tease with their tangled grace,
As rhymes waltz off to a silly place.
Imagine a poem where the words run fast,
And laughter is the present that's meant to last.

So come join the fun, don't be shy,
Let your tongue play as the phrases fly.
In the soft embrace of language we find,
A hilarious bond that tastefully binds.

## Enchanted Fragrance

In gardens where scents pirouette,
Flowers whisper secrets you won't forget.
Roses boast of their lovely flair,
While daisies tease with a sun-kissed stare.

Lavender laughs in her soothing hue,
Jasmine's giggle is sweet and true.
But lilies, oh lilies, cannot be beat,
With an aroma that dances on every street.

Dandelions puff with a huffy pride,
As marigolds play, side by side.
Petunias chuckle with petals so bright,
Creating a symphony of scents at night.

So breathe in the joy, let laughter unfurl,
In every aroma, there's magic to twirl.
Each whiff a story, a fragrant jest,
In the enchanted realm, we are truly blessed.

## Rich Sprouts

In a garden where sprouts are full of cheer,
Tiny veggies whisper, 'Come over here!'
Radishes tease with a spicy punch,
While carrots just giggle, crunch by crunch.

Peas pop open, full of sly grins,
Saying, 'Life's a feast, come join in!'
Lettuce laughs in a leafy embrace,
Waving at beans in a playful race.

Cucumbers smirk with their cooling jest,
While broccoli claims he's the veggie best.
Tomatoes blush in the warm sun's glow,
As radishes play tag and steal the show.

Join the sprout party, it's never a bore,
Where greens bring joy and so much more.
With laughter and growth, let's sprout our dreams,
In this rich, funny garden of whims and schemes.

## Flourish and Flow

In garden beds where veggies chat,
The carrots brag, 'We're really fat!'
Tomatoes blush in summer's kiss,
While radishes root for a lettuce bliss.

The daisies gossip, what a show!
Their tales of butterflies on the go.
Sunflowers smile, with heads so grand,
As bees sweet-talk across the land.

Composting dreams of worms' delight,
Turn scraps to gold, what a sight!
With every weed that dares to bloom,
We laugh and dance, dispelling gloom.

So as we grow in mirth and cheer,
With veggie puns that we hold dear,
Let's raise our shovels high above,
And doubtless cultivate our love!

## Serene Hues

The violets whisper in a breeze,
Drooping petals, oh, such a tease!
Lavenders joke about their scents,
While wind makes sure it all's intense!

A daffodil dons a sunny hat,
Saying, 'Guess what? I'm where it's at!'
Tulips giggle as they take their stand,
In colorful clusters, quite unplanned.

One rose says, 'Don't be so coy!'
While marigolds shout, 'Let's spread the joy!'
Nature's palette, bold and bright,
Takes a jab at the moonlight night.

In this garden, laughter's sweet,
As petals dance on tiny feet,
With every hue and every joke,
Life's just a giggle wrapped in smoke.

## Harvest of Words

In fields of prose, where stories grow,
Each word a seed, planted in rows.
A pun springs up like weeds in spring,
While metaphors dance, oh what a fling!

The novelist sips on coffee bold,
While characters do what they're told.
Plot twists tumble like falling leaves,
As humor twitches like spider's weaves.

A haiku hops, with playful rhymes,
Sonnet stretches, it takes its time.
In this harvest, each line's a feast,
Feeding minds, the laughter's increased.

So gather round, dear friends, and share,
Your quirkiest thoughts, if you dare!
With words like veggies, growing fast,
Let's cultivate fun, make moments last!

## **Linger in Petals**

In gardens bright, where picnics reign,
The ants throw parties, quite insane.
With crumbs of cake and lemonade,
The flowers giggle, unafraid.

A bumblebee serves drinks on cue,
While daisies have a subtle view.
Lilies lounge, enjoying the sun,
They whisper tales of silly fun.

The flowerpots make secret pacts,
And swap their gossip with some acts.
A hedge betrays the kitchen's scent,
While butterflies laugh, so heaven-sent.

So linger here, in petals bright,
Where laughter blooms, and hearts take flight,
In nature's joy, we twirl and sway,
And dance through flowers, come what may!

## **Rhythms of Growth**

In the garden where weeds throw a ruckus,
A daffodil dances, looking quite circus.
The carrots are gossiping, rolling with laughter,
While tomatoes debate who's the first in the chapter.

Bees buzz in rhythm, a buzzing ballet,
They tango with petals, all on display.
The sun, like a DJ, spins vibrant tunes,
As nature's own party begins in full bloom.

Basil sneezes loudly, the irony's ripe,
As mint shows off in her new summer stripe.
The veggies all giggle, no need to be meek,
In this garden of joy, it's fun all week.

So come join the harvest, don't be a pest,
For laughter's the fruit that we all love best.
In this patch of delight, joy grows with intent,
It's nature's own circus, a grand event!

## Blooms of Emotion

The roses are blushing, they just spilled some tea,
While daisies play matchmaker, giggling with glee.
Ivy's climbing high, dreaming big of romance,
And violets whisper, 'Give love a chance!'

Tulips wear sunglasses, strutting with flair,
While sunflowers nod as if they're in prayer.
Petunias put on a comedic charade,
As lilies stand tall like they're in a parade.

Worms tell long tales, they twist and they twine,
While roots high-five each other in time.
Weeds try to join in, but nobody braves,
The laughter erupts, as the daisies wave!

Amidst all the giggles, love's fragrance is found,
In the comedy club where the blooms gather 'round.
Where the garden's a stage, and each flower's a star,
With jokes that sprout freely, near and afar!

## Nature's Lyrics

In the forest, the trees tell jokes from the past,
As squirrels plot mischief, they're having a blast.
Frogs croak out sonnets, with rhythm and rhyme,
While crickets compose, keeping perfect time.

The river is giggling, splashing with glee,
Making funny faces, for all to see.
Fish swim in circles, like they've lost their way,
Chasing bubbles that pop, brightening the day.

Clouds drift in laughter, puffing up high,
Pretending they're sheep, floating by in the sky.
The wind whispers jokes, tickling the ear,
Turning the quiet into raucous cheer.

Nature's a bard, crafting tales from the ground,
In this theatre of life, joy always is found.
With every new bloom and each giggle they share,
The earth keeps on singing, with plenty of flair!

## **Dripping with Metaphor**

The raindrops are scribbles from clouds holding pens,
Writing stories of growth, where the fun never ends.
Each puddle's a canvas, where splashes are art,
And worms are the poets, all playing their part.

The sun's a loud joker, playing hide and seek,
While shadows are sidekicks, all sly and chic.
Leaves flutter like pages in a wind-swept debate,
As branches entwine to examine their fate.

Creativity blooms in this garden of jest,
Where laughter's the language that we all love best.
With every new droplet, fresh fun we uncover,
As metaphor drips from nature's sweet cover.

So dance in the rain, let the joy freely flow,
In this world of bright metaphors, laughter will grow.
With trees as our chorus and skies as our tune,
Let's revel in nature's funny festoon!

## **Celestial Harvest**

Up in the sky, where the veggies float,
Carrots are dancing, and peas wear a coat.
With potatoes that giggle, and radishes cheer,
They throw a grand party, it's that time of year.

Cucumbers waltz in a twirling spree,
Zucchini's the DJ, spinning tunes with glee.
Tomatoes are juggling, it's quite a sight,
Under the moon, they party all night.

Cherries in bonnets, grapes in a line,
Laughing together, they sip on sweet wine.
The corn on the cob makes the silliest face,
As pumpkins roll in with a jolly warm grace.

Toasts with some salsa, cheers echo far,
Veggies unite, and they're raising the bar.
With laughter and spices, they twirl, jive, and sing,
A harvest celestial, where joy is the king.

## Digesting Delight

In the land of munchies, where flavors reside,
Beans tell a tale while the tacos confide.
Pasta performs, pirouetting with flair,
But bread rolls dispute who has the best hair.

Salads all chatter, dressed up so fine,
Dressings are flirty, like, "Hey, that's divine!"
While olives gossip, sharing each quirk,
Potatoes just sit, like, "I'm not here to work!"

Sushi's a ninja, it rolls with a kick,
While donuts are cheerleaders, sticking a trick.
Ice creams are giggling, melting away fast,
Inventing a dance that can't help but last.

With laughter and crunching, it's quite the delight,
As plates pile up high, what a glorious sight!
In this merry banquet, full of such cheer,
Each bite is a giggle; oh, bring on the beer!

## Plump Phrases

In the quirk of fruit, where humor is ripe,
Peaches are poets, they drum up the hype.
With apples in glasses, they raise a fine toast,
Declaring that laughter deserves to be boast.

Bananas, they slip, and the crowd starts to roar,
"Don't slip on our lines; we've seen this before!"
Berries in clusters, with wit that can charm,
They wrap up their punchlines, oh, never a harm.

Citrus remarks with a zesty little grin,
"Let's squeeze out the joy, let the fun times begin!"
While pineapples sway, wearing crowns oh so proud,
Their tropic-flavored puns draw in quite a crowd.

So gather your fruits for a literary feast,
Where silly is savory, laughter increased.
In this orchard of wit, let your heart take flight,
With plump little phrases, we'll party all night!

**Fruits of Inspiration**

Once in a kitchen, where dreams sprout and grow,
Fruits plot their antics, all in a row.
A berry brigade with their capes made of fluff,
While bananas play tricks, saying, "This is tough!"

Mangoes suggest, "Let's start a rock band,
With rhythm so juicy, we'll be in demand!"
But apples retort with a crisp little quip,
"No one can handle our juicy backflip!"

Grapes form a line, and they dance in the air,
While oranges juggle, not a moment to spare.
"Who's the best fruit? Let's settle this now,"
But everyone's laughing; they don't know how.

Together they giggle, with zest that's sincere,
Inspiring each other throughout the whole year.
With laughter as sweet as their luscious delight,
These fruits have the fun that just feels so right.

# Tales of the Tilled Soil

In the garden, worms take a stroll,
With radishes wearing a leafy bowl.
Tomatoes gossip all day long,
While carrots croon their secret song.

A lettuce capers, a peas' grand dance,
Zucchini takes a rather bold chance.
Pumpkins don hats and strut with pride,
While onions giggle, trying to hide.

Earthworms are plotting some mischief tonight,
They're scheming to steal the stars' twilight.
All while the compost sits cocooned,
Making jokes that leaves are marooned.

So raise a toast to the garden cheer,
Where laughter flourishes, let's give a cheer!
For in the soil where the silliness grows,
A crew of veggies in comedy glows.

## Nectarial Narratives

Bees tell tales with a buzzing hum,
Of flowers flirting, a pollination drum.
Hummingbirds sip with a cheeky grin,
While sunflowers spin, reveling in sin.

Butterflies flaunt in colors so wild,
Dancing like children, carefree and mild.
The blooms gossip about scents so sweet,
While daisies dispute who has the best seat.

A clover's wish is to dance in the breeze,
While violets tease about making cheese.
Lavender joins in with a winking flirt,
"Don't worry, dear weeds, we won't get hurt!"

So raise a toast to nectar-filled chats,
In the garden where laughter begets.
For each tiny petal, so sly and spry,
Is weaving a story that'll make you sigh.

# Song of the Seeds

Seeds gather round for their nightly sing,
Dreaming of roots and the joy they bring.
Radishes boast of a spicy flair,
While beans do the cha-cha in fresh garden air.

Cornbellies nuzzle with a husky grin,
"Who needs sun when you've got a whimsical spin?"
Chilies chuckle, their heat aglow,
While peas declare, "We're the stars of the show!"

Pumpkin seeds whisper, "Let's have some fun,
We'll roll down the hill when the day's done!"
As kale tells jokes with a rugged face,
"Life's so much better with a leafy embrace!"

So listen close to the seeds' jovial glee,
In the soil where hilarity runs free.
For every sprout, a giggle or cheer,
In this garden of laughter, year after year.

## Petal-Flecked Dreams

In moonlit nights, petals weave their dreams,
With whispers of fragrance that moonlight beams.
Tulips in taffeta curtsey and sway,
While roses plot a fabulous play.

Dandelions chuckle, a joke in the air,
As violets gossip without a care.
A daisy yells, "I'm the queen of this scene!"
While pansies argue, "I'm the best green!"

Lily pads join in with an aquatic splash,
While irises grumble about a fast flash.
"Who needs the sun? Let's light up the night,"
Squeaks a comet with a dazzling flight.

So dream away in this petal parade,
Where laughter and joy are blissfully made.
For in each colorful bloom, what a swirl,
The garden's alive with whimsy, a twirl!

## Abloom in Thought

In a garden of dreams, thoughts take flight,
Wiggly worms dance under the moonlight.
Petals giggle, secrets they keep,
While bees plot mischief, not losing sleep.

Dandelions chuckle, proud as can be,
As daisies roll their eyes, oh, can't you see?
A cactus in flip-flops, strutting about,
While roses throw shade, just a tad pout.

Sunflowers waltz, tall and bright,
While lilies argue, who blooms just right?
In this playful patch, humor's the theme,
Nature's a joke, or so it would seem!

With laughter and cheer, the flowers sway,
In a floral ballet, they dance and play.
Each petal a punchline, each leaf a jest,
Abloom in thought, this garden's the best!

## Earthy Inspirations

Mud pies and giggles, a childhood mess,
A worm's little wiggle, nature's finesse.
Compost and laughter, compost and smells,
Tales from the soil, where the humor dwells.

Beneath the thick surface, where roots intertwine,
A chorus of crickets sings punchlines so fine.
Roses so rosy, in bloom and in blush,
While thorns feel neglected, oh, what a rush!

Wacky weeds twisting in curious ways,
Telling tall tales of bright sunny days.
Pebbles chime in with a jangly laugh,
Declaring themselves as nature's good staff!

In soil we find wisdom, in dirt we find fun,
Each seed a potential burst of a pun.
Let laughter take root, let silliness sprout,
In earthy inspirations, joy is devout!

## Vagal Dances

Wiggle your leaves in the breeze with glee,
While branches do jiggle, come dance with me!
Funky ferns flourish in a rhythm divine,
While pinecones shimmy, oh how they shine!

Dizzy daisies twirl, in colorful spins,
Sunbeams are backstage, where the fun begins.
Vagal snakes slither, with rhythms so groovy,
As twigs tap their toes, feeling all movie!

Bamboo's tango, a slick little sway,
While tulips burst forth, excited to play.
Insects with maracas join right on cue,
Nature's so witty, it's all quite the view!

Around and around, the flora does whirl,
Even rocks in a conga, give it a twirl.
Laughter's the tune that we all like to hum,
In vagal dances, let the fun come!

**Growth and Glory**

Sprouting up funny, in colors so bright,
Petunias with pom-poms, it's quite the sight.
Buds of ambition, they reach for the sky,
With humor in bloom, let's give it a try!

Curling vines giggle, climbing so high,
As seedlings swap stories, oh me, oh my!
A daisy in glasses, looking so wise,
While poppies wear hats, to everyone's surprise.

Nature's a circus, with laughter so grand,
Each leaf a performer, a playfully planned.
Roots dive deep, in the soil they explore,
Seeking out mischief, oh, who could ask for more?

So let us take note, in this playful spree,
Growth comes with chuckles, so wild and free.
In the garden of humor, we bloom with delight,
In growth and glory, life's simply just right!

## The Garden's Cadence

In the garden where the carrots sway,
Bees buzz louder than the kids at play.
A tomato tripped on its own fine vine,
Said it was just practicing to dine.

The lettuce danced a wiggly jig,
While radishes laughed, oh so big!
Spinach wore shades, looking quite cool,
While peas conspired, the mischievous school.

Dandelions giggled, wearing their crowns,
Telling the roses they're just shooting clowns.
Bunnies hopped in, with a cheeky smirk,
Claiming they'd come for the veggies' quirk.

And though they bicker on whose is best,
They all know together, they're truly blessed.

## Vivid Vignettes

In vivid hues, the flowers play,
Petunias gossip about the day.
A daffodil sneezed—now that's quite rare,
Its pollen sprinkled everywhere!

Zinnias boast of their sunny thrills,
While marigolds bask in fancier frills.
A sunflower tried to strikingly pose,
But tripped on its stem, oh, woes on woes!

A rogue cucumber flirted with bees,
Begging them sweetly to take it, please!
With every sweet smile, it swayed anew,
As daisies rolled eyes and chuckled too.

The garden's wild laughter echoed around,
With petals and leaves on wobbly ground.

## **Blooms in Starlight**

Under stars, where the moonlight glows,
The daisies plot mischief, right on their toes.
Roses giggle, with thorns tucked in tight,
As night unfolds with floral delight.

Peonies whisper secrets so grand,
While violets organize a band.
A tulip sneezed, and what a show,
It sneezed confetti! Oh how it glowed!

Carnations went skating on the dew,
Flower pot parties, oh what to do!
A buttercup spilled all its sweet tea,
Sipping on laughter, feeling so free.

As petals unfold to the night's song,
In a patchwork of laughter, they all belong.

## Sips of Serenity

In a cup of sunshine, the herbs do steep,
Lavender giggles, oh, isn't it sweet?
Mint whispers tales of summer delight,
While chamomile snores in the warm twilight.

Basil sprinkles laughter with zest,
Thyme joins in, claiming it's the best.
Sage shakes its head like a worried sage,
Amused by young herbs acting their age.

A hibiscus dreamed of a glamorous brew,
While roses debated if tea time was due.
Lemon balm danced, ready to sip,
As they twirled to the music on a joyful trip.

With every sip in this herbal spree,
Laughter mingled with tea, wild and free.

## Echoes of Eden

In Eden's realm, fruits giggle and sway,
Naughty apples whisper, 'Come out and play!'
Peaches flaunt their fuzz, so bold and bright,
While berries gossip under the moonlight.

Radishes dance, in their leafy attire,
Proudly they prance, fueled by desire.
"Look at us," they chirp, "we're crunchy and fun!"
While carrots roll over, under the sun.

Oh, how the garden throws a grand bash,
With cucumbers laughing, while radishes flash.
Lettuce in hats, dressed for the affair,
Tomorrow, they claim, will be even more rare!

So, come join the feast in this playful mirth,
Where veggies conspire for all they're worth.
In echoes of Eden, let's dance and sing,
For ripe, fruity laughter is the best thing!

## Radiant Refrains

In a patch of daisies, a snail takes its time,
Singing sweet refrains, in a rhythm and rhyme.
Butterflies flutter, on a mission so grand,
While sunflowers sway, in a carnival band.

"Hey there, Mr. Beetle, care for a race?"
But he chuckles back, "I'm stuck in this place!"
With leaves full of laughter, how can we frown?
When nature's our muse, we lose all our crowns.

Pepper plants chuckle, in whimsical tones,
Waving their stems, as they dance with the drones.
"One more salsa, and we'll take home the prize!"
While marigolds cheer, with their bright, sunny eyes.

Oh, the garden's alive with its quirks and delight,
As critters and blossoms spark joy every night.
In radiant refrains, let the giggles resound,
For laughter in whispers is what we have found!

## Whirling Wisps of Green

In a whirl of green, the chives start to twirl,
With the peas in a line, ready to hurl.
Over the patch, the wind gives a call,
Let's dance all together, we're having a ball!

The lettuce is laughing, a crisp little chap,
Bouncing with glee, wearing nature's best wrap.
While radishes dig, in a game of hide and seek,
Who knew gardening could be this unique?

Brownies bake treats, with strawberries on top,
Swirling and twirling, we'll never stop.
With vines tangled up in a chaotic embrace,
Everyone's joining this green, funny race!

Oh, let's frolic and giggle, 'neath skies so serene,
In a garden so jolly, and bursting with green.
Whirling wisps of mirth bring a shine to our day,
As laughter and joy come out to play!

## Tapestry of Flora

In the tapestry's weave, unique blooms arise,
Petals paint stories under vast, azure skies.
Daisies are jesters, with crowns made of cheer,
While thorns play the role of the edgy, austere.

"Why so prickly?" a pansy did tease,
"Join us for laughs, take it down with ease!"
The cosmos giggle, adorned in their hue,
With a wink at the daisies, they shine and renew.

Bees buzzing tunes, in a musical spree,
Sipping on nectar, as sweet as can be.
Lush leaves and petals, all chuckling with glee,
In this floral circus, come laugh wildly free!

So here's to the flora, with their quirky flair,
Painting the garden with colors we share.
A tapestry woven with giggles and song,
In this vibrant paradise, we all belong!

## Colors of the Mind

Bright blues and greens, oh what a scene,
They twist and they twirl, like a jelly bean.
Yellows burst forth, making us grin,
While reds play peek-a-boo, inviting us in.

Swirling imaginations dance on the page,
Each hue a giggle, a whimsical sage.
Pinks tickle fancies, make laughter abound,
In this silly palette, joy can be found.

## **Petal-Powered Poetry**

Oh, flowers are chatting, gossiping loud,
Roses in red, they're drawing a crowd.
Tulips tell secrets, with a wink and a sway,
While daisies roll laughter, come out to play.

Forget-me-nots giggle, don't want to fade,
In a garden of puns, where humor's displayed.
Take a stroll down the path of some playful prose,
Join in the laughter, let your spirit compose.

## **Harmonies from the Earth**

The soil sings songs, oh what a delight,
Worms break the rhythm, wiggle left and right.
Roots tap-dance quietly, under the sun,
While daisies join in, having such fun!

A chorus of crickets, they keep up the beat,
Bees are the backup, buzzing so sweet.
Nature's own band, with a whimsical twist,
You can't help but smile, how can you resist?

**Dew-kissed Verses**

Each drop of dew is a sparkle of glee,
Whispering secrets to you and to me.
They twinkle and laugh, when the sun shines bright,
Painting the world in a glistening light.

The grass giggles softly, swaying in cheer,
While blossoms join in, bringing good cheer.
In this frosty moment, where laughter's accrued,
We dance on the dew, with joy that's renewed.

## Lush Verses of Nature

In gardens where the critters play,
A gnome for tea, or so they say.
The daisies giggle, share a rhyme,
While crickets dance to beats of thyme.

The sun throws light, a spotlight bright,
On bees in bow ties, what a sight!
They sip from blooms in fancy style,
And leave their buzzing, cheeky smile.

The trees wear hats of leafy flair,
And squirrels prank with nutty air.
The flowers pose, they strike a grin,
Nature's runway, let the fun begin!

With every breeze, a laughter rings,
While butterflies play on paper wings.
In this wild dance where quirks unite,
Nature's humor feels just right!

## Petals and Poetry

A petal fell, it slipped and swayed,
The rose's secret dance displayed.
'Twas stamped upon, a comical plight,
As blooms, they laughed in pure delight.

The tulips wear their hats so tall,
Declaring spring's grand floral ball.
With every thump, they stomp and prance,
These petals sure know how to dance!

The lily pads serenade the pond,
With frogs that croak like they're quite fond.
They hold a concert, offbeat and wild,
As insects groove, nature's adopted child.

With verses spun from nature's heart,
A whimsy world where giggles start.
In petals bright, we find our jest,
In this green realm, we're truly blessed!

## Odes to Opulence

In gardens lush, where flavors tease,
A carrot dons a coat with ease.
The squash is suave, it struts with flair,
While potatoes play the debonair.

The lettuce flaunts its leafy dress,
With radishes, they dine to impress.
They sip from cups of dew and cheer,
A banquet grand, with jokes sincere.

The herbs parade, they twirl and spin,
Dill's got the moves, it's quite the win!
With thyme in hand, they serve a jest,
An opulent feast, nature's best!

In blooms of gold, they toast and laugh,
Whispering secrets of their craft.
In every leaf, a tale untold,
Where laughter reigns in green and gold.

## Verdant Whispers

Amidst the ferns where giggles bloom,
A squirrel plots, and oh, that zoom!
With acorns dressed in tiny ties,
They host a tea with secret spies.

The grasses hiccup in the breeze,
While daisies shout, "Oh, do you please!"
They play their games of hide and seek,
With butterflies that flirt and peek.

In whispers soft, the willows sway,
As dragonflies join in the fray.
They spin and twirl, a waltz so spry,
In verdant dreams, they leap and fly.

A laughter loud, it fills the glade,
As nature's jesters dance and fade.
In every whisper, joy sings sweet,
In this green realm, life's not discreet!

## Nature's Palette

In a forest filled with paint,
Trees all laugh and start to faint.
One wore stripes, another dots,
Squirrels chuckle, tying knots.

Flowers dance in vibrant hues,
Bumblebees sing silly blues.
Colors clash like socks on feet,
Nature's art, funny and sweet.

The clouds join in with polka spots,
While rainbows dance with silly thoughts.
A cheeky sun winks with a grin,
In this gallery, love does begin.

Laughter echoes, birds take flight,
Nature's humor shines so bright.
With every leaf and every tree,
A masterpiece of glee, you see!

## Whispers of the Wild

The owl hoots jokes from high above,
While rabbits giggle, oh how they love!
The winds carry whispers of delight,
As the moon plays tricks with its silver light.

Squirrels debate the best nut snack,
They stumble and tumble, fall on their back.
Raccoons search bins for hidden treats,
In the wild, life's funny feats!

A bear in shades takes a sun-soaked nap,
Dreaming of honey, caught in a trap.
While deer in suits plan grand affairs,
Hilarity rules; it fills the airs.

Through giggles of the breezy pines,
Nature's humor sways and shines.
With every rustle, a laugh we find,
In whispers of the wild, perfectly lined!

# Dreamy Orchards

In orchards rich with fruits so bright,
Apples giggle, a comical sight.
Pears wear hats, like pirates' gold,
Telling tales that never grow old.

Cherries chuckle while hanging around,
Their laughter echoes without a sound.
Plums stack up, ready to race,
Rolling down with style and grace.

Beneath the branches, bees are slick,
Joking around, buzzing quick.
Each fruit a character, each branch a friend,
In playful gardens, joy has no end.

With every wind that sways the trees,
Laughter floats upon the breeze.
Dreamy orchards, a fanciful spree,
A whimsical world, happy and free!

## Love Among the Leaves

Two trees swayed in a dance of glee,
Whispering secrets for all to see.
Branches tangled, hearts in a knot,
Leaves giggled softly, oh what a plot!

Amidst the ferns, a pair of snails,
Shared sweet stories, left funny trails.
With slimy kisses beneath the shade,
Nature's comedy never fades.

A couple of frogs croaked out romance,
Jumping around in a moonlit dance.
As branches rustle with joy and cheer,
Love among the leaves, year after year.

In every petal, in every sigh,
A touch of laughter flutters by.
Here in this world where the heart believes,
Laughter blooms amid the leaves!

www.ingramcontent.com/pod-product-compliance
Lightning Source LLC
Chambersburg PA
CBHW051657160426
43209CB00004B/932